MILITARY MACHINE FACT FRENZY!

by Cari Meister and Matt Doeden

CAPSTONE PRESS
a capstone imprint

Published by Capstone Press, an imprint of Capstone
1710 Roe Crest Drive, North Mankato, Minnesota 56003
capstonepub.com

Military Machine Fact Frenzy! was originally published as *Totally Amazing Facts About Military Sea and Air Vehicles* and *Totally Amazing Facts About Military Land Vehicles,* copyright 2017 by Capstone Press.

Library of Congress Cataloging-in-Publication Data is available on the Library of Congress website.

ISBN: 9798875254727 (hardcover)
ISBN: 9798875254673 (paperback)
ISBN: 9798875254680 (ebook PDF)

Summary: There's a MILITARY MACHINE FACT FRENZY headed your way! Did you know that there are military machines called "Whispering Death," "the Aardvark," and even a "military jet ski"? Or that an F-15 Eagle can land with just one wing? Dozens of bite-size facts are paired with incredible photos of mighty military machines. Whether kids are in the mood for a quick look or an absorbing read, they're sure to learn some fascinating facts about military tech, vehicles, and science as they blast through these pages.

Editorial Credits
Designer: Jaime Willems; Media Researcher: Svetlana Zhurkin; Production Specialist: Whitney Schaefer

Image Credits
Alamy: Abaca Press, 46 (top), 47, Hannu Mononen, 53, Johnny Saunderson, 34, PJF Military Collection, 52 (middle), 55, 62; Associated Press: CP, Kevin Frayer, 32; Bridgeman Images: © Look and Learn, 63, Reuters/Ali Jarekji, 35; DVIDS: Courtesy Photo, 1 (bottom), 5 (top), 24, Lockheed Martin photo by Andy Wolfe/Cmdr. Victor Chen, 7, Regional Command Southwest/Sgt. Keonaona Paulo, 13, U.S. Air Force/Photo by Airman 1st Class Julia Lebens, 19 (back), U.S. Air Force/Photo by Airman 1st Class Matthew Seefeldt, back cover, 17, 64, U.S. Air Force/Photo by Capt. Joshua Thompson, 1 (top), 11, U.S. Air Force/Photo by Samuel King Jr., 10, U.S. Air Force/Photo by Senior Airman Noah D. Coger, 18, U.S. Air Force/Photo by Staff Sgt. Brian Kelly, cover (top right), 6, U.S. Air National Guard/Photo by Staff Sgt. Riley Johnson, 16, U.S. Army National Guard/Photo by Capt. Brian, cover (top left), U.S. Army National Guard/Photo by Capt. Brian Hare, 22, U.S. Army/Photo by Christopher Kaufmann, 25, U.S. Army/Photo by Markus Rauchenberger, 39, U.S. Army/Photo by Spc. Christian Cote, 38, U.S. Army/Photo by Spc. Joyce Avila-Collazo, 23, U.S. Marine Corps/Photo by Lance Cpl. Julien Rodarte, 40, 41, U.S. Marine Corps/Sgt. Christopher Q. Stone, 26th MEU Combat Camera, 12, U.S. Navy/Photo by Chief Petty Officer Keith DeVinney, 60, U.S. Navy/Photo by Lt. j.g. Mary Kierstead, 49, U.S. Navy/Photo by Mass Communication Specialist 3rd Class Aleksandr Freutel, 48, U.S. Navy/Photo by Mass Communication Specialist 3rd Class Travis J. Kuykendall, 4 (middle), U.S. Navy/Photo by Petty Officer 2nd Class Conor Minto, 61, U.S. Navy/Photo by Petty Officer 3rd Class William Sykes, 56, U.S. Navy/Photo by Seaman William Bennett IV, cover (bottom right), 59; Getty Images: ratpack223, 50, Stocktrek/Vernon Lewis Gallery, 27; NARA: 21, U.S. Air Force, 15; Newscom: ZUMA Press/Barratts, 14; Shutterstock: Alexandre.ROSA, 29, Andrii Vodolazhskyi, 51, CkyBe (speech bubble), cover and throughout, Daverse, 4 (right), Edoma, 30, Elyasaf Jehuda, 42, Everett Collection, 26, Flying Camera, 31, gn8 (rays and lines), cover and throughout, Gorobets, 19 (coins), InsectWorld, 20, JeremyShow (military icons), cover and throughout, Lana Praded, 46 (bottom), Le Do, cover (bottom left), makarenko7, 4 (left), 43, Mariusz Lopusiewicz, 58, Nazarii M, 3, 28, Ninevija, 57, Reimar, 33, Reytr, 52 (bottom), v_kulieva (gradient background), back cover and throughout, vadimmmus, 5 (bottom), 45; U.S. Air Force: Air Force Research Laboratory/Courtesy artwork, 9, Photo by Tech. Sgt. Kregg York, 8; U.S. Navy: Naval Sea Systems Command, 54, Photo by PH1 Arlo K. Abrahamson, 36, 37

Printed and bound in China. PO 6461

TABLE
OF
CONTENTS

MILITARY MACHINE MANIA

The world's militaries have come up with some amazing vehicles and machines designed to protect, defend, and attack. Some by land, some by air, some by sea . . . and some by all three! Get ready to discover fascinating details about military machines, the creative technology that made them possible, and the brave people who operate them!

1000
PREPARE FOR TAKEOFF . . .
AND AMAZEMENT!

MACHINES IN THE SKY

F-35C LIGHTNING II—UNITED STATES

The F-35C Lightning II is a supersonic fighter plane with a top speed of about 1,200 miles (1,930 kilometers) per hour. (That's faster than the speed of sound!)

The F-35C's wings fold up so it takes up less room on the deck of the aircraft carrier.

The F-35C is a stealth plane. Its materials and shape are built so radar from enemies can't spot it.

WINDRACERS ULTRA DRONE—UNITED STATES

The ULTRA (Unmanned Long-endurance Tactical Reconnaissance Aircraft) is an Air Force drone that can fly for more than 2,000 miles (3,200 km) without refueling.

The ULTRA has a wingspan of more than 80 feet (24 meters). It can carry up to 400 pounds (180 kilograms) of cargo.

THIS DRONE USES RADAR AND OTHER LONG-RANGE SENSORS TO WATCH THE LAND BELOW IT.

MH-139 GREY WOLF—UNITED STATES

The MH-139 Grey Wolf entered U.S. Air Force service in 2020. It can be used for security patrols, to carry cargo, and in search-and-rescue missions.

This helicopter can carry 15 people, five medics and all of their gear, or two M240 7.62mm machine guns.

Two PT6C-67C turboshaft engines power the MH-139. Its large rotors measure 45.2 feet (13.8 m) and give it lift.

AV-8B HARRIER FIGHTER JET—UNITED STATES

The Harrier is the only fighter jet that can take off and land vertically.

The jet can fly more than 630 miles (1,010 km) per hour!

Its massive turbofan engines are made by Rolls-Royce.

BRISTOL BEAUFIGHTER, "THE BEAU" —UNITED KINGDOM AND AUSTRALIA

Almost 6,000 Beaufighters were built between 1940 and 1946.

The Beau was called "Whispering Death" by the Japanese because the engines were so quiet.

Its quiet engines and radar system made this plane a stealthy nighttime fighter.

WOW!

THE F-15 IS A REMARKABLE AIRCRAFT IN EVERY WAY. IT CAN LAND SAFELY WITH ONLY ONE WING!

It has a perfect record: zero air combat losses.

The F-15 can successfully shoot down satellites.

B-2 BOMBER—UNITED STATES

The B-2 is covered with a special paint that makes it almost invisible to ground-based sensors.

In 2003 Jennifer Wilson became the first female pilot to fly the B-2 in a combat mission.

One B-2 Bomber costs about $2 billion.

THE FOKKER DR.1—GERMANY

The Fokker Dr.1 was a triplane—it had three wings!

No original Fokker DR.1s exist today. Only copies do.

Manfred von Richtofen, the "Red Baron," was the most feared German pilot of World War I (1914–1918). He flew a Fokker.

BOEING CH-47D CHINOOK—UNITED STATES

The Chinook helicopter can lift 19,500 pounds (8,845 kg)!

CHINOOKS ARE VERY RARELY RETIRED. THEY ARE FIXED INSTEAD.

One pilot who fought in the U.S. War in Afghanistan (2001–2021) flew the same Chinook that his grandfather flew more than 50 years earlier in the Vietnam War (1955–1975).

MACHINES ON LAND

M10 BOOKER—UNITED STATES

The M10 Booker was briefly in U.S. Army service in the 2020s. It is a light tank—a combat vehicle that is smaller and faster than a full-sized tank.

The M10 Booker is loaded with powerful weapons. It has machine guns, grenade launchers, and a 105mm M35 gun that sits on top of the tank.

The M10 was named for two U.S. Army soldiers who died in combat: Private Robert D. Booker in World War II (1939–1945), and Staff Sergeant Stevon Booker in the Iraq War (2003–2011).

MARK 1 TANK—UNITED KINGDOM

Used in World War I (1914–1918), Mark 1 tanks came in two versions: the "male" and the "female." The "male" tank weighed a little more.

The tank was loud, and fumes from the engine often made the crew sick!

It was such a beast of a machine, it took four people to drive it.

THE BUSHMASTER—AUSTRALIA

The Bushmaster armored vehicle has special tires. Even if the tires are punctured, it can keep going.

THE BUSHMASTER CAN RUN FOR UP TO THREE DAYS WITHOUT STOPPING!

It takes only one person to drive it, but it has room for up to nine other people.

SD.KFZ.2 KETTENKRAD—GERMANY

Need a tow? The Kettenkrad could tow planes on an airstrip.

This machine was half tank, half motorcycle!

Germany used it in World War II (1939–1945). After the war, farmers used it as an ATV (all-terrain vehicle).

Coyote Reconnaissance Vehicle—Canada

The Coyote armored vehicle is a high-tech spy machine.

This vehicle has radar infrared video surveillance. It can detect vehicles up to 15 miles (24 km) away.

The Coyote is only about 21 feet (6.4 m) long, but it weighs more than 14 tons (12.7 metric tons).

AARDVARK JSFU (JOINT SERVICE FLAIL UNIT)–UNITED KINGDOM AND UNITED STATES

The Aardvark is a mine-flail vehicle. It clears a path of mines by detonating them. The rear flail has 72 chains with striker tips.

Special soundproofing in the cab keeps the crew in a near-silent environment.

Crews are safe in this beast! No crew member in the vehicle has ever been hurt when flailing live mines.

CHENOWTH SCORPION DPV (DESERT PATROL VEHICLE)—UNITED STATES

The Scorpion is like a pumped-up dune buggy.

Navy SEALs and other soldiers have zipped around in the Scorpion during desert wars.

WOW!

IT CAN GO 200 MILES (322 KM) WITHOUT REFUELING.

M270 MLRS (MULTIPLE LAUNCH ROCKET SYSTEM)

The United States, France, Italy, West Germany, and the United Kingdom were all involved in the development of the M270.

The M270 can fire 12 rounds of rockets in 40 seconds.

Its ballistic missiles can hit targets 186 miles (300 km) away. That's about the distance from Washington, D.C., to Trenton, New Jersey!

MAARS (MODULAR ADVANCED ARMED ROBOTIC SYSTEM)—UNITED STATES

This remote-controlled surveillance and reconnaissance tool has seven different kinds of cameras.

Besides spying, the MAARS can set explosives, open doors, and remove unwanted objects with a special "claw."

WOW!

ALTHOUGH THE MAARS IS TOTALLY HIGH-TECH, IT'S SUPER SLOW. ITS MAXIMUM SPEED IS 7 MILES (11 KM) PER HOUR.

MERKAVA—ISRAEL

Watch out! Unlike some tanks, a Merkava can fire at moving targets while also moving.

The Merkava 4 has a thermal shroud on the gun. The shroud keeps the barrel from overheating and bending.

AIRCRAFT CARRIERS BY THE NUMBERS

SHIP	COUNTRY
USS *Gerald R. Ford*	United States
Admiral Kuznetsov	Russia
HMS *Queen Elizabeth*	United Kingdom
Charles de Gaulle	France

LENGTH	AIRCRAFT CAPACITY	CREW
1,092 feet (333 m)	90	4,500
1,000 feet (305 m)	52	1,500
965 feet (284 m)	72	679
857 feet (261 m)	35–40	1,200

MANTA RAY UUV (UNCREWED UNDERWATER VEHICLE)—UNITED STATES

The U.S. Navy's Manta Ray is an underwater drone shaped like the fish it was named for.

The Manta Ray has no crew. It can go places that are too dangerous for crewed submarines. It doesn't even need anyone to steer it remotely—it drives itself.

The Manta Ray can dive thousands of feet underwater. It anchors to the ocean floor and powers down most of its systems. It can stay that way for days at a time, "hibernating."

ZUMWALT-CLASS DESTROYER–UNITED STATES

The Zumwalt-class destroyer is a stealth U.S. Navy ship that holds 197 sailors. It's the largest surface attack ship in the world at 610 feet (186 m) long.

It is also very expensive—each one cost around $8 billion to build! So the Navy ordered only three of them.

This destroyer is built for attack. It uses the Tomahawk missile to attack targets on land, and it can carry an MH-60R Seahawk helicopter.

U-BOATS—GERMANY

During World War II (1939-1945), more than 3,000 civilian and Allied ships were sunk by U-boats.

U-boats were very complicated. They had many handwheels inside that were used to control pressure levels.

Most U-boats had emblems. The U-47's emblem was a snorting bull.

FS *MARJATA*—NORWAY

The FS *Marjata* is one of the world's top spy ships—and it's shaped like a pizza slice!

Its main job is to spy on the Russian military in the Arctic Sea.

It's so sophisticated that few people know everything it can do. We do know that it has the most high-tech spy gear around.

SEA SHADOW (IX-529)—UNITED STATES

The IX-529 was the world's first stealth ship.

Only one was ever built, and the U.S. Military never really used it. They sold the *Sea Shadow* for scrap in 2012.

The ship in the James Bond movie *Tomorrow Never Dies* was based on the IX-529.

Hovercrafts ride on a cushion of air and are made to land troops on beaches.

Russia and Ukraine have the largest military hovercrafts. Each one can carry three battle tanks!

At high speeds, modern hovercrafts leave almost no wake.

USS *NEW YORK* (LPD-21)—UNITED STATES

The USS *New York* is a type of amphibious warfare ship called a "landing platform dock" (LPD).

Its bow was made with 7.5 tons (6.8 metric tons) of steel from the World Trade Center buildings fallen on 9/11.

The ship's motto is: "Strength forged through sacrifice. Never forget."

LCS (LITTORAL COMBAT SHIP)—UNITED STATES

The LCS is the U.S. Navy's newest class of warship.

WOW!

ALTHOUGH THE SHIPS ARE SMALL, THEY CAN GO 40 KNOTS (46 MILES/74 KM) PER HOUR!

Former Commander John Kochendorfer called it, "The coolest ship out there. A military jet ski with a flight deck and a gun."

BY SEA AND AIR ... OR NOWHERE?

The de Lackner HZ-1 Aerocycle (United States) was designed in the 1950s to be a "flying platform," but the project was canceled after there were too many testing crashes.

The Convair F2Y Sea Dart (United States) fighter jet, created in the 1950s, didn't need a runway. It had hydro-skis for takeoff and landing on the ocean! Sadly, during one of its test flights, it disintegrated. It was never used in service.

BOOKS IN THIS SERIES